I0309548

WE CAN DO IT! – A JOURNAL (COLLEGE RULE)
MORDANT MEDIA JOURNALS

We Can Do It!

A Mordant Media Journal

WWW.MORDANTMEDIA.COM

COLLEGE RULE

ISBN- 13: 978-0-9971795-7-6
ISBN-10: 0-9971795-7-0

MORDANT MEDIA ™©®
A Division of Charlton Productions

We Can Do It!

We Can Do It!

We Can Do It!

We Can Do It!

We Can Do It!

We Can Do It!

We Can Do It!

We Can Do It!

We Can Do It!

We Can Do It!

We Can Do It!

We Can Do It!

We Can Do It!

We Can Do It!

We Can Do It!

We Can Do It!

We Can Do It!

We Can Do It!

We Can Do It!

We Can Do It!

We Can Do It!

We Can Do It!

We Can Do It!

We Can Do It!

We Can Do It!

We Can Do It!

We Can Do It!

We Can Do It!

We Can Do It!

We Can Do It!

We Can Do It!

We Can Do It!

We Can Do It!

We Can Do It!

We Can Do It!

We Can Do It!

We Can Do It!

We Can Do It!

We Can Do It!

We Can Do It!

We Can Do It!

We Can Do It!

We Can Do It!

We Can Do It!

We Can Do It!

We Can Do It!

We Can Do It!

We Can Do It!

We Can Do It!

We Can Do It!

We Can Do It!

We Can Do It!

We Can Do It!

We Can Do It!

We Can Do It!

We Can Do It!

We Can Do It!

We Can Do It!

We Can Do It!

We Can Do It!

We Can Do It!

We Can Do It!

We Can Do It!

We Can Do It!

We Can Do It!

We Can Do It!

We Can Do It!

We Can Do It!

We Can Do It!

We Can Do It!

We Can Do It!

We Can Do It!

We Can Do It!

We Can Do It!

We Can Do It!

We Can Do It!

We Can Do It!

We Can Do It!

We Can Do It!

We Can Do It!

We Can Do It!

We Can Do It!

We Can Do It!

We Can Do It!

We Can Do It!

We Can Do It!

We Can Do It!

We Can Do It!

We Can Do It!

We Can Do It!

We Can Do It!

We Can Do It!

We Can Do It!

We Can Do It!

We Can Do It!

SEE OUR LARGE SELECTION OF JOURNALS ON AMAZON.
WWW.AMAZON.COM/AUTHOR/BAERCHARLTON

FOR BULK ORDERS, CONTACT US AT
INFO@MORDANTMEDIA.COM

~ ~ ~

BAER CHARLTON, PRODUCTION DESIGN
LAURA REYNOLDS, ART
ROGENA MITCHELL-JONES, LITERARY EDITOR

MORDANT MEDIA ™©®
A Division of Charlton Productions

www.ingramcontent.com/pod-product-compliance
Lightning Source LLC
Chambersburg PA
CBHW060500010526
44118CB00018B/2489